Horse Coloring Book

Horse Coloring Pages For Kids

ISBN-13: 978-1973896050
ISBN-10: 1973896052
Copyright © 2017 Tanya Turner
All rights reserved.

No part of this publication may be copied, reproduced in any format, by any means, electronic or otherwise, without prior consent from the copyright owner and publisher of this book.

Made in the USA
Las Vegas, NV
28 July 2022